D0907535

Mirrors of my Soul

A Collection of Life's Poetry

ELLEN ALBAN

Note for Librarians: a cataloguing record for this book that includes Dewey Decimal Classification and US Library of Congress numbers is available from the Library and Archives of Canada. The complete cataloguing record can be obtained from their online database at:
www.collectionscanada.ca/amicus/index-e.html
ISBN 1-4120-4375-1

This book is printed on acid free paper.
Cover Design and Page Layout by Bonnie Toews
Edited by Ellen Beck
Printed in Victoria, BC, Canada

TRAFFORD

Offices in Canada, USA, Ireland, UK and Spain

This book was published *on-demand* in cooperation with Trafford Publishing. On-demand publishing is a unique process and service of making a book available for retail sale to the public taking advantage of on-demand manufacturing and Internet marketing. On-demand publishing includes promotions, retail sales, manufacturing, order fulfilment, accounting and collecting royalties on behalf of the author.

Book sales for North America and international:
Trafford Publishing, 6E–2333 Government St.,
Victoria, BC v8t 4p4 CANADA
phone 250 383 6864 (toll-free 1 888 232 4444)
fax 250 383 6804; email to orders@trafford.com

Book sales in Europe:
Trafford Publishing (uk) Ltd., Enterprise House, Wistaston Road Business Centre, Wistaston Road, Crewe, Cheshire cw2 7rp UNITED KINGDOM
phone 01270 251 396 (local rate 0845 230 9601)
facsimile 01270 254 983; orders.uk@trafford.com

Order online at:
www.trafford.com/robots/04-2183.html

10 9 8 7 6 5 4 3 2

Prayer for the Millennium

To all the dear women assembled here tonight
My hope is that my prayer is a candle burning bright
To simply wish for health, happiness and peace
Is certainly part of my prayer
But we all need much more
So that with true hearts and souls
We will the new millennium explore
Our strength in adversity
Open arms to the needy
Loving ourselves richly
As we all deserve
Loving others with sincerity
As is their need
Reaching out to ease pain
Healing ancient rifts
Teaching our children and grandchildren
The priceless value of commitment
Learning to accept the inevitability of change
Aging gracefully with acceptance and wisdom
Imparting our knowledge to those willing to learn
Inspiring others through stories of our life experience
When called bearing the inevitable with grace
Leaving our legacy of love
To those dear ones who remain

These, my dear ladies, are my prayers for the Millennium.

ELLEN ALBAN

Dedication

This collection of life's poetry

is dedicated to my

dear family and friends,

and to all who are

living with

Parkinson's Disease

Contents

Introduction

Seven years ago I was diagnosed with Parkinson's disease. I had been living on overdrive for many years, as had so many newly "liberated" women of the late sixties. I had a teaching position at a local high school and a young family. Those years were busy, but nothing like what would later transpire.

At age thirty-three, I became responsible for helping three elderly members of my family. Over the next fifteen years, my grandmother, my mother and my stepmother all needed me to assist them in many ways. By the time I reached forty-eight, they had all passed on. It seemed as if I would now have a modicum of spare time. But almost immediately a new challenge presented itself.

On a weekend getaway, our friend Earl Dobkin, a family physician in Toronto, noticed a slight tremor in my right hand. He suggested to my husband that I see a neurologist as soon as possible. Could this happen to me at what seemed to be such a young age? Yes, of course it could. And it did. I accepted the news calmly. After all, I had been through so much already. I would have to deal with this new challenge one day at a time. Eight years later, that is exactly what I am still doing.

At the time of my diagnosis, I realized that I would have to de-stress my life as expeditiously as possible and face the fact that my teaching days were numbered. In February 1996, I took a leave of absence for six weeks, thinking that I might rest and soon return. But I never have.

Instead, I resolved to begin looking at my life in a different way and to try things I previously thought were impossible. I began with beading necklaces, bracelets and eyeglass chains, and then tried my hand at watercolor, a medium that doesn't seem to care if the painter's brush is being held by a tremoring hand. Each hobby was so enjoyable that I found myself immersed for days at a time in one and then the other. I recommend each of these to all who wish to awaken their artistic side. But there was much more to come.

One day I decided to purchase a pretty spiral notebook and begin to write a journal. Instead of writing about my days, I began to write poems, poems and still more poems. Over the next three months, I filled six spiral notebooks with many poems that described my life, my experiences and my feelings.

It became imperative to learn how to use the computer, and although I am far from being an expert, I use my computer daily.

Poems began accumulating at an astounding rate. No subject was off limits. From talking pasta pots to headless mannequins, to ladies who lunch, anything was and is possible in my work.

The more I write, the more I become a student of life and the human condition. With each experience I feel deeply, inhale the positives and expunge the negatives. In all, I know that I am continuously evolving and I take great joy in that knowledge.

Why does someone like me decide to reveal her thoughts, feelings and viewpoint to the world? Perhaps to make others think about their own vision, to leave a legacy for my friends and family, or even to inspire others to think that they, too, are capable of much more than they can imagine. Or perhaps this desire has always been buried so deeply that it took these many years to discover and take the risk of exposing my word paintings to the scrutiny of other eyes, hearts and minds.

I would like to thank everyone who helped and encouraged me in my endeavor. My friends, my family, and most especially Bonnie Toews and Susan Pearl, who made me feel that I could inspire others, and that I should do so.

Sections of this book are divided into themes as reflections of the soul on various topics of relevance to understanding nature, life, people, relationships, and the nature of the creative process. Did I ever believe that I could write these words? No. But with Bonnie's inspiration, 'all is possible' became a mantra for my life.

Thank you everyone, for taking the time to read, to reflect, to remember and to rejoice in the knowledge that we are not alone on our journey through life, but are accompanied by challenge, struggle and hopefully triumph.

To poetry and to Life!

ELLEN

REFLECTIONS

ON

THE SOUL

Soul Connection

My soul is a mystery masked inside
I know it exists but it loves to hide
It only appears when I sleep or rest
When are my soul and I
Going to discuss for us what's best?

Perhaps I must wait patiently
Surrender to the powers that be
In hopes that someday
My soul and I will be as one
For then we will fly!

Soul Food

Powerful rhythms, piano, drums
Strings, create a magical hum
Brass and percussion enhance the mix
Deep emotions themselves affix

The music dances without repose
Galloping through treble and bass
Like a wild horse riding the wind

Racing madly to a triumphant finale
Instruments meld in their ultimate union
Listeners enraptured

The audience sighs —
Silence after exquisite highs
Hands meet, pleasures abound
All rise, applaud this musical round

Earth and Soul Motion

Waves breaking on the sand
In, out, back, forth
Phases of night and day
Full, half, slender moon
Sunrise, sunset, twilight, darkness

Feelings in the human heart
Crash against the fragile soul
With bitter, tender, cosmic reality
Imagining, creating, celebrating
Destroying, mourning, rebuilding

The Prayer Circle

Twenty-two loving women
Write a special prayer
For the Millennium
In a circle prayers are read
Put into the Tibetan bowl
Chants of God and love
Fervently sung
Light, love and positive energy
Pervade this place
Tears are shed
Hearts are lifted
Bonds are created

Soul Power

I am the mistress of my soul
I play different parts in my role
Sometimes sweet, occasionally sour
Often witty, rarely dour

No one can live my life for me
No one discerns what I see
No one lives inside my brain
No one knows my deepest pain

No one understands if I say
"I don't really feel like that today"
 My thoughts belong only to me
Therein lays their exclusivity

Soul Garden

The narrow fieldstone path
Leads into the enchanted garden
Of my peaceful being
Each natural formation
Creates a unique design
From one stone to the next I tread
Carefully, lightly, consciously
For this magical garden must be savored
By all my heightened senses

But on the stones, silent witnesses to eternity
Nothing dares to grow
Only faded gray hues exist
Surrounded by nature's brushed floral landscape
Sparkling in the early morning mist
Where are the abundant feeders, the white gazebos?
Where are the twenty faithful monarchs?
When will they ever appear?

Ghosts

Ghosts of the past
Inhabit us all
In character, emotions
Talent and faults
In speech, voice
Language and style

But these phantoms cannot replicate
A bygone soul's existence

The past creates the present
And for that we give thanks and prayer

The Silence Within

Silence bombards acute ears
Sit, contemplate, and excavate
The innermost regions
Transcend the scrub
Unearth the essence
Buried in the core of humanity

Music of the Spirit

Born from gentle notes of the harp
Peaceful chords of the guitar
The fragile spirit is summoned

A world where music is food, air, and water
To choked parched souls

A world where peace wields absolute power
And friendly clouds float

An azure sky
Where benevolent sunbeams heal with musical rays

Ephemeral Mist

An old man bends forward
To sit in his favorite rocking chair
Mist settles on the damp earth
Embracing the ground
Stretching above the evergreens
Shrouding earth and all its beings
With its mysterious opaque veil
An obscure yet wondrous sight
For aging, awestruck eyes

The long, cool night
Creeps into its hiding place
Making room for daylight
The ephemeral mist embraces earth
Vanishing in the land
Alive with its simple natural tones
Part of the world
He *thinks* he understands

Revived Souls

Death lurks
Amidst the pristine beauty
Of a winter's day

Souls fractured, legs broken
Human and beast
Tormented and maimed

Life perseveres
Amidst horror, pain
Blood, disfigurement, loss

Redemption
In the endless space of Montana

Hearts rejuvenated
Soul mate and kindred spirit

Greatness

The greatness of humility is by all admired
The modesty of brilliance one never tires
The kindness and generosity of simple souls
Fill the heart with wonder and represent new goals
The beauty of silence is like a woman's lovely face
But when words destroy its mystique
Secrets are erased
An invisible wall between people
The height of ugliness
Breaking down human barriers
Is possible only when love and kindness
Are honestly expressed

Heaven's Honour

When families are bereft
From a mother's passing
Shock and abandonment
Quickly surface
If the mother of herself
Has generously given
The loss is that much
Greater to bear

Where to find comfort?
Imagining our mothers
In God's special celestial heaven
Reserved for those who, while on earth
Have truly sacrificed
Indeed a special group
God knows their generosity to others
Their unfailing support

Dear Families,

Know that God takes extra care of mothers
In his heavenly space and prayers

REFLECTIONS

ON

MIDDLE AGE

Middle Aged and Moving

Dyed hair, a tremor, and laugh lines
Accompany her on her daily visit
To the dance studio
Where a huge mirror reflects her every move

Some bleary-eyed witnesses notice nothing
Except their coffee cups in their firm grasps
Others stroll leisurely in and out
Lost in early morning thoughts and plans

A few take notice of the running shoe dancer
And slyly glance at the scene
Is she a ballerina 'wanna be'? A Tai Chi refugee?
A chacha-tango-waltzer devotee?

Most cannot understand her compulsion
At the barre in front of the mirror
Enveloped in her own world
The inner child is bursting with pride

Changing Times

About twenty years ago we moved in
With a desire for order our only sin
Now we two inhabit so many spaces
Filled with memories and aging faces

Along the way we found treasures for décor
Were given others, acquired more and more
One day we looked around with great surprise
Our simple home had assumed a new disguise

For over the years we had collected with pride
Much more than our first gifts as groom and bride
Our abode was now pleading for some simplicity
After thirty-three years there was no room to breathe

Slowly we began the task with much hesitation
Will we ever need these items for donation?
We tried not to dwell on that possibility
Instead we decided to let it go and see

We now feel less burdened by material things
And look ahead to what our new life brings

Dead From the Neck Up

I'm dead from the neck up, I suppose
I noticed I'm wearing ripped panty hose
I'm dull as dishwater, slow as molasses
I'm up my tree, I've lost my glasses

Where are my keys, my hat, my coat?
I can't believe I've got my own goat
It's a senior moment; I pause and think
Of what I needed; Stop! I'm into the drink

The bubblies bring me such relaxation
That I forget where I want to go on vacation
I read that book; you know, the most recent tale
Of our favorite author -- she just got out of jail

I'm resting for a moment and then I'll go upstairs
To get all the items needing special repairs
On my way I stop and think, where did I hide that bubbly drink?

All of a sudden I realize the error of my ways
I pop all my pills as dawn changes into day
I'm alive and kicking; I'm a feisty grand dame
My teacher is experience; life is my game

Perfection

I am only average in height and weight
I am sometimes in a sorry state
I'm a brunette with gray in my roots
I'm imperfectly perfect — in size 10 boots!

I'm a little lumpy around the waist
Where gravity's pull cannot be erased
I'm a little freckled from the sun
I'm imperfectly perfect — but into fun!

I love chocolate, jam, and French fries
My zest for life I cannot disguise
I'm a gal of vision, inside and out
I'm imperfectly perfect — that's what I'm all about!

If you look inside my mind and heart
You'll see a real person, just for a start
One who has felt life's deepest sorrow
But one who always believes in tomorrow

I'm imperfectly perfect — that's what I say
And I hope I'll always remain that way!

Love Questions Itself
in Middle Age

Foreboding, shaking, wanting, forsaken
Heaviness of heart, sadness, doubts, fears
Stupidity, naivety, cruelty, silence
Sweetness, shivers, eyes that finally see
Or do they, can they, will they ever?

Pitter-patter of heartbeats
Forbidden thoughts
Forbidden dreams
Forbidden feelings

Empty Nester

Where once a space for baby lives
With crayons, play dough, wooden blocks
Toddler squabbles, giggles, baby talk

Short years later the metamorphosis occurred
A child's desk, bookcase, MAC, or clone
Now this spot is all alone

Teenage life invaded with its own dreams
Mixed with their tears and frustrations
Now it's time for future creations

Floating

I float fearlessly on a thick cloud
Forgetting former tempests
Determined to find my own universe
By charting my own course

But bravado quickly evaporates
As long dead issues are reborn
In my search for new answers
I dig endlessly into the unknown

I hack away at poisons in my mind
Push forward to reach the golden heart
At last I understand; all pain is fleeting
Beauty is life and life is beauty

Into Middle Age

Brown-gray tones
Atop hazel eyes
Overlooking small shoulders
Big boobs
Slim arms, legs, feet
Carry me along
Into middle age
Squeezing my brain daily
For orange creativity
For steadiness of hand
For confidence in me

Unknown Journey

Bubbles blown into the air
Travel afar
If they dare
Floating about with ease
On a warm July breeze

Childhood feelings in my adult bones
Bubbles floating into the unknown

In the Fifties Zone

A time in my life with challenges galore
When I think I can't take on any more
The nest becomes empty, its rooms bared
Of the latest gossip, tears, giggles shared

What to do with this gift, a visible embrace?
Spread my clothes into sweet free space?
Create my long awaited desert island bliss?
I am now blessed with a spatial kiss

Refurbish with my hopes and desires
Savor the thrill of what transpires
Create what I wish, retreat with pleasure
Here my soul feels joy beyond measure

Fifty-One

Fifty-one means
Menopause, grown up offspring
Trying new things
Knowing how to love

Believing in Spirit
Cheering up others
Walking in the country
Feeling grateful

Family, birthdays
Good friends, good food
Boisterous laughter
Soothing sun

Fifty-one means
Taking nothing for granted
Celebrating Life!

Blocked

I stare at the blank screen
Hoping for the idea
The verbal sizzle
That will transport me
On my literary voyage
Where I show others
My view of the human condition
And find myself in the process

The Women of the 21st Century

We are the women of the age of technology
Our advancement into a man's world undeniable
Our intelligence and ambition without parallel
Our determination to succeed overwhelming
Our confidence growing with each achievement

Into a world of fast food, lean cuisine, vanity sizing
We march aerobically, lift weights, run marathons
Espouse the virtues of slender slinky sexy bodies
Size two the answer to our ever-present yearning
To be desirable, beloved, as we tiptoe into middle age

But at this point the waters become muddy
We're fraught with anxiety, divorce
Wrinkles, crow's feet, weight gain
Relationships evolve, renew, or dissolve as lives play out
Ideas once espoused are now seen as naïve, fallacious
The perfect life must exist, but exactly where is a mystery

We, the women of equal rights, have voted in two careers
Instead of the one that used to consume all our time
Proud, accomplished, driven to be all and do all
We stagger into the future with heart attacks and strokes
Our companions, dynamic, liberated, overwrought women

Aren't we wonderful?

I Am At War

I am at war
Against self doubt
Against fear
Against jealousy
Against injustice
Against hypocrisy
Against cruelty
Against hatred
Against evil
Against prejudice
I am at war

I Am At Peace

I am at peace
With who I am
With how I feel
With my body
With my family
With my friends
With strangers
With nature
With the seasons
With the stars
I am at peace

Take Me as I Am

Who am I? One might need to ask
A secret soul under a public mask
They only know what eyes can see
But I hope that's never all of me
Beneath there's much more to explore
So I'll unlock each separate door

What does the world want to know?
My dress size, my age, where I go
To shop for clothes, my weekend recreation
My meal plans and my latest vacation?

A tall slim woman responds to such queries
As best she can, but very soon wearies
No one takes the time to truly understand
Her thoughts, her dreams, her passionate stand

They simply accept what they wish to believe
Even though the physical can much deceive
I keep my sweet secrets inside my heart
Until one unique mind sets itself apart
Can she accept what's under the mask?
Her simple reply: "Did I even need to ask?"

The New Face of Sixty-Five

The lady with the curls quietly speaks
Her opinions daily we all seek
She's often busier than a beehive
She's the new face of sixty-five

She's been one of us for many a year
With her we've laughed and shed a tear
She's devoted, kind, and her talent thrives
She's the new face of sixty-five

At home she's not about to retire
Helping children and grandchildren
Her sweetness shines, she's vibrantly alive
She's the new face of sixty-five

But that's the rub, you can easily see
For she doesn't even look fifty-three!
To be like her, we must all strive
For she's the new face of sixty-five!

Old

What do you see when you look at me?

Wrinkles, jowls, blotchy skin?
Thin hair, glasses, false teeth in?

Look again — with kindness in your heart

What you now see is a sculpted work of art
Its canvas wisdom, empathy, grace
The result of time's work on a human face

Now it's my turn to look at you

Freshness of youth, smooth white skin
Bright sparkling eyes, contact lenses in

Now I see what you cannot truly hide

You have not yet learned humility
An indifferent heart, superficial concerns
Selfishness abounds, jealousy burns

I ask, "Who would YOU rather be?"

REFLECTIONS

ON

ANIMALS

The Elephant Danced

An elephant loved to dance his own way
And decided to learn more by taking ballet
When he arrived at the ballet school
The teacher said that his body was not cool
"You're too large and ungainly to do well in ballet
Look, the giraffe is lean; you're not built that way"
But the elephant knew that he wanted to dance
So he begged the teacher to give him a chance
"Well, all right, you can stay in my group
But watch what we do; stand tall, don't stoop!"

The elephant was so eager to learn this skill
That he stretched on from his toes, such will, such will!
The teacher, surprised, asked how did he know
How to move his great body with such graceful flow?
The elephant replied that it was all deep inside
That he wanted to dance, and felt himself glide
"You'll be my star pupil; you're one of a kind"
And the elephant smiled, for she had been blind

First Robins

At dusk the cool April air
Suddenly came alive
With a spirited symphony of robins
Chirping travelers returning
To nest in northern climes

We listened and marveled
At the rhythms of their instinct
At their devotion to their journey
At the melodies of their conversation
At our childish joy in their presence

Butterfly

Dancing with delicate moves
On wings of warm autumn wind
The butterfly flutters weightlessly
Its patterns designing the air

But the dancer herself
Is Nature's best composition
In orange with black trim
Melding beauty with grace

Her destination is instinctive
Along the genetic journey
Movement and form entwine
The result......perfection

A Squirrel

On a windy cold November afternoon
With the patio doors reflecting the sun
I suddenly noticed an overstuffed squirrel
Deep inside my summer plant pot

He stopped, knowing other eyes were watching
I, too, became still; two different species
Feeling each other's presence
Who would win, he or I?

A minute dragged on, as each waited
In anticipation of a bang on the glass
No response, then "GO AWAY!"
But nothing happened; we stood our ground

Suddenly a head turned and I saw those eyes
Grey blue, not chocolate brown as I had imagined.
A long fluffy tail following his torso
As he jumped out of my summer plant pot

Before he finally faded from view
He glared at me antagonistically
I crouched in the light, mesmerized
We had shared one brief moment in time

The Mouse

It was midnight at the cottage
I felt his presence there
Waiting to make his brazen appearance
With villainous joy, he left his mark everywhere
On my favorite sofa and chair
In the sink, on the counter
Just about everywhere

What chutzpah!
How dare he invade my private space!
Live here rent-free
In the lap of cottage luxury!
How dare he think my food is his
And sample anything — even my Cheez Whiz!

I know why he prefers my rural home
To the vast outdoors, his terrain to comb
But beware, little one
Numbered are your gourmet snacks
With peanut butter and a custom trap
I'll lie in wait to hear the sound SNAP!

The Cottage Raccoon

To our dear little cottage raccoon
Your nocturnal visits always spell doom!
The residue you casually deposit there
We must clean and scrape, but you don't care!

We know you love our barbecued meats
That we carefully protect from your paws and feet
We want you to live happily outside
So please find another place to reside!

Praying on my Mind

She was only a pet, some might say
Those for whom a strand of hair on a sofa
Might spoil their perfect home and orderly day

She greeted all with a wagging tail
And jumped on each lap, licked innocently
Announced with a bark the arrival of the mail

Sometimes a fresh stain was found on a mat
And the swishing tail overturned many a cup
All she wanted was a gentle loving pat

The puppy stage passed and now she knew
Friends and family and places she could go
Even tricks to perform when we wanted her to

At first only a pet, no depth or humanity
Until one day we noticed with much surprise
That she could truly feel and see

She understood sadness with a caring presence
She knew when problems weighted our souls
She felt our troubles and knew their essence

"Only a pet!" you might exclaim in disbelief
Yet so intuitive in every unique situation
Patting her gave us a sense of relief

So it was that we took her for granted
She would live forever, we tried to believe
Until one day we listened when she panted

"How could this happen?" we wanted to know
As she lay at the vet's with tubes everywhere
She was our puppy, our kin; must she now go?

Only an animal? How you presume to know!
How can a four-pawed creature cause such a stir
Live fifteen years with a faithful pet
I guarantee you'll be sad and your eyes will blur

The Awakening

Stretched out on an old soft terry towel
The perfect portrait of canine relaxation
Taffy lies in a state of complete trust
In her surroundings, in her being, in me

I stare, transfixed, at this wonder of nature
From which I can learn by quiet observation
Her even breathing, contented constitution
Eyes often open, silently observing the sameness of her
environment

Suddenly an unexpected bang destroys our stillness
Taffy surges into active pursuit of its source
With an aggressive bark, a seldom used growl
Four insistent paws alert me to potential imminent danger

Our moment, now shattered by unforeseen events
Reveals Taffy's protective instinct
Her loyalty, courage, quick wit, intelligence
All emanate from my ten-pound poodle companion

The Power of the Butterfly

Oh, to be free like the weightless butterfly!
Oh, to wend one's way from southern to northern climes
And back again as seasons change
Migration of magnificence and strength
Singular beauty in the summer landscape
What mystery surrounds this lengthy odyssey?

Fish Tails

A strong silver fish swam in the aquarium with pride
All knew the agility in his wide finny stride
One day he noticed a female glowing nearby
She wiggled, giggled, smiled, and said "Hi"

Around him in circles with nary a plan
She danced as she swam and spoke "fish" and "man"
One day they smiled and many bubbles exuded
As the tank was their oyster and they were included

The next morning the female looked pale and felt ill
One of her schoolmate's lives was now still
The silvery male reached out with his fin
For he knew deep down what shape she was in

With that first bubble blown on to her cheek
She knew that much lay inside his fish speak
Soon they exchanged bubbled thoughts and dreams
Of jumping from ponds and romping in streams

Other fish friends didn't even stop to stare
For they were busy creating their own special pair
They didn't notice these two in their lovelorn state
Even though their special feelings did clearly resonate

REFLECTIONS

ON

ILLNESS

Ache in the Pit

Ache in the pit
Weight in the chest
Water in the eyes
Crack in the heart

Tremble in the fingers
Mush on the brain
Frown on the lips
Much pain, explain

Bruise to the spirit
Death in the soul
Rainbow on the horizon?
The answer is NO.

The Joy of Falling

Soft, fluffy descent
Into temporary oblivion
Head tilts heavily
Lids droop, weighted down
Deftly drawn into sleep's depths
Muscles release tension
Succumb to the inevitable pull
Of the illusory world of dreams

Circle of Healers

Round and round, the energy intensifies
As we embrace the push and pull of light
Whose power sears through thick clear crystals
Clutched firmly in our sweaty, pulsating palms

Silence, intuition, light, vibration
Interwoven as we mothers pray
For our own divine Mother Earth

Our thoughts infuse one another
Our circle of eight transcends boundaries
As invocations catapult into planetary acceptance

Sun, moon, stars, all watch in awe
As the People of the Light, the Eights
Glorify their universe with prayers of love

One Tiny Pill

One ivory pill for an energized state
One white pill so the tremor will abate
One blue pill to restore my calm
One pink pill to place in my palm

One round pill to strengthen my bones
One cod liver pill to keep my thoughts toned
One yellow pill to lubricate all my parts
One more pill and the whole process restarts!

Hills and Plains

The barren hills hold no song
No echoes of voices now or then
No firs or pines to soften the vista
No bubbling of a steamy spring
No silky moss to blanket the earth

The plains can only stay silent
Witness to nothing
Remaining as they have always been
Flat, dry, uninhabitable, inhospitable
Beloved by no one and nothing

Victorious Pain

Invincible
We courted illness
Broke the rules
Pushed the limits
Yearned to accomplish more
Forgetting our fragility
Ignoring weakness
Imagining a perfect, pain-free existence

Engulfed by new companions
Worry, grief, stress
Abandoned by former allies
Peace, silence, meditation.
War ongoing, pain victorious
Lives forever changed

Wall

Inside my heart you stand tall and proud
Preventing my truth from speaking aloud
Inside my body your light beams red
Detachment results; I'm almost dead
Inside my soul your lease is forever
Until I ask, am I worthy of this endeavor?

Wherein lies the answer to my query?
From an ego that must resolve to be cheery
I will destroy your powers one by one
My heart speaks clearly; it finds the sun

I will now put you out on the street
My hope is that we ne'er again meet
I feel the rush of blood to my head
My wholeness IS; I refuse to be dead

Evil Emotion

I lie in wait for tortured souls
Bodies, minds, spirits in distress
To divert them from their goals

I work until I've chipped away
At self worth, until
Only tiny remnants dare to stay

Under my huge black wing
Illness slowly grows
Day and night my deadly beacon glows

As resistance fails I gloat with success
I'm evil, I'm great
I'm the source of frustration and hate

When I finally rear my ugly head
Human beings will wish they were dead

Anxiety

Anxiety
The 21st century demon
Possesses all who search daily
For house and car keys
Who worry about
Stolen purses and wallets
Who obsess each morning
About numbers, salaries, bills
Taxes, expenses
Who cry over dress sizes
Low fat food, wrinkles
Who despise exercise
Soy, gray hair, age spots
Who over-analyze relationships
With friends, spouses, children
Who fear obtaining or retaining a job
Being promoted
Who dread going to school
Writing tests and exams
Making the grade
Who feel utterly helpless
In steering their own course
Thus, invisible irrational negativity
Becomes the norm

Help!

REFLECTIONS

ON

REFLECTIONS

Universal Power

Music floating on wings of air
Invisible, powerful
Melody wafting into pleasant interludes,
crescendos

All becoming one in the spirit of the universe
I sit, listen, watch and wait
Absorb, relax, feel, create

Uneasy Thoughts

Tranquil Sunday afternoon
Thoughts racing in my head
Panting in bizarre animation

For they crash like whitecaps
On a deserted northern coast
Until they find their niche

How misled I must really be
To imagine my silence pensive
Such naïve stupidity!

Reinvention

Change your clothes
Change your car
Change your career

Change your mate
Change your friends
Change your values
Change your religion

Change your hair
Change your nose
Change your teeth
Change your eyes
Change your skin color

Change your dress size
Change your image
Change your disguise

Change leaves nothing
Change is not you
Change destroys

The essence of you
Gone, gone...gone

Choose

Choose to be
Choose to grow
Choose to learn
Choose to go slow

Choose to laugh
Choose to feel
Choose to cry
Choose to be real

Choose your spirit
Choose your way
Choose your friends
Choose your pastime for this day

Choose your life's path
Choose to play
Choose to be carefree
Choose to rejoice in every way

Awareness

Rigidity passed
Spontaneity its replacement
Living fully in the moment
Experiencing the wonder of now
With its aromas of beauty
Its sounds of touch
Its tastes of immediacy
Its textures of silk, cotton, lace, wool
Its scents of dried leaves, coffee
Bubbling apple pie
Awareness is becoming clearer
Under the indigo sky
Dotted by the ethereal moon
Surrounded by diamond stars

Mirror

Reflecting pool on the wall
Impartially unveiling my truth
Gray hair, crow's feet
Bags, freckles, blotches

A muted light transforms
Softer lines, smoother surfaces
Warmer tones, whiter teeth
A self-confident aura appears

But your limited visual power
Makes true discovery impossible
Thus my essence remains pristine
Sun-filled, glorious, triumphant

Forgiveness

Mix one cup of insensitivity
With a dash of stupidity
And a tablespoon of misunderstanding
Stir until well mixed
Irrational resentment rises
To the top of the mixture
Simmer in the mind and heart
For several months
Refusing to add or remove
Other emotions from the mix
Ignore all loving, caring and apologetic gestures
Do not in any way alter the recipe
No matter how much poison seeps
Irrevocably into body, mind and soul
Do not tolerate explanations of any kind
Know that this version is the only one possible
Do not forgive; remain inflexible

Introspection

Look inside the pit
Deep, dark, insidious
You'll now descend
Passing smiles on the wall
Friendships, some abandoned
Sinking into family conflict
Descending into blue moods
Changing to black outlooks
Now arriving at depression
Attempted suicide, hospitalizations
And the Truth at the end of it all

Today

Today

Sun, clouds
Rain, wind
Calm, storm

Today is Life
Highs, lows
The winds of Change

Inescapable
Unforgiving

Today
Nothing is permanent

Neither good nor evil
Hate nor love
Poverty nor riches

The only constant
In Life
Is Change

Eternal Trap

If life is a circle
I'm living in a square
Unable to escape
My spirit's wear and tear

If life is a square
I'm trapped by four walls
My soul is stripped bare
Wandering naked in halls

If life is a triangle
I'm choked in my brain
But the rest of my being
Has too much free rein

If I were free
Without any bars
Words couldn't fail
They'd fly to the stars!

Fire Dance

The dance of fire is rapid
Whirling enthusiastically
On an intense searing trajectory
Towards Death
Choking black fumes
Its ugly trademark
It forges ahead relentlessly
Encompassing all in its dark lethal path
Ahead lay only Fate and Inevitability.
The fire has attained its ruthless goal

Helping Others

Is it possible to be of service
To others in need of support
When one's only aid
Is the power of the written or spoken word?

Can one help heal the pain of others
In this seemingly simple way?
Or is it self-important to believe
In one's own verbal healing powers?

With the touch of a caring hand
A compassionate arm around a shoulder
A reassuring hug and kiss
Maybe anything is possible

A Mind at War

Can a mind at war with itself
Relax to let its ideas gently flow?
Can the psyche be unfettered
And able to grasp life's truths?

In Time lies the answer
Time to meditate
Time to exercise
Time for music
Time for yoga
Time for solitude

Now thoughts can swirl freely
Through the channels of the mind
Attaining depths as yet undiscovered
Peace the sweetest result

Cool

Cool, clear spheres encased in a mesh bag
Click in neighborly embrace
Each is identical to the next
The lifetime attraction of glass perfection

A child's game played on bent knee
At school or at home, a competition ensues
Fingers work adroitly, skill wins
Winner takes all; loser cries in vain

"I've got all my marbles!" You know what it means
But in old age one may play with marbles again
And some will slyly ask, "Has he lost all his marbles?"
And the answer will be "He lost them long ago
But found them again"

Brief Escape

Warm inviting water
Sun and shade melding
Bodies surfacing and bobbing
Happily in the morning heat

Up and back
Under and over
Round and about
Splashing boisterously

An hour flies by
Gone is the peace
Time to readjust
Time to move on

Be Whoever
You Are

Be grateful
Be happy
Be generous
Be productive
But most of all
Be yourself

Don't be envious
Don't be rash
Don't be arrogant
Don't be thoughtless
Most of all
Be yourself

War Prayer

My dearest family,

May you never know the smell of war
An entire society ravaged by civilized dictatorship
Starving, disbelieving, immobilized
Tattered ballet slippers, operatic screams
Echoing in deserted barren mansions

My dearest,

May your banquet halls never be headquarters
Where maps rule sovereign
Their deathly scepters aimed at damning multi-
directional destinies
Choked, suffocating, ceaseless labor
Mass annihilation, merciful cremation

Dearest ones,

Do you now begin to understand?

Passion

It burns white hot
Slashing mediocrity into nothingness
Propelling promise into achievement
Artistry unveils Truth, ignites thought
Engenders delight in a human heart

Unique Vision

In the reflection of the mirror
I see a sad girl
With freckles, zits, pudgy cheeks
Hiding from her world

Out of the torment of childhood
I feel inner strength enveloping me
As maturity, generosity, empathy
Reflect the 'me' of here and now

Out of the crises of adulthood
I suffer cruelly until I learn
That rolling with Life's punches
Is the only way I'll survive

From the aroma of spring flowers
I inhale the blessing of maturity
Feeling regenerated in my soul
Loving every instant of it all

Regret

I am Regret
In life I'm a major player
My iron grip will overwhelm your mind

I imprison people in errors of long ago
I rehash their weaknesses without mercy
I trick their souls into believing my truth
I am the cause of their deepest remorse

My power stops the Present laden with welcome gifts
My grasp on the past is tight
I destroy all filaments of love and support
They are my adversaries

I imprison you in the past and hide the keys
Escape me if you dare endure the pain
Of squeezing through the black iron bars
Escape me if you dare pry apart my teeth

Fulfillment

Soil, loam, earth, fertility
Color, fragrance, texture, beauty
Hands, eyes, fingers grasping
Enjoying labor's pleasure
All seemingly overwhelming
But in that moment unseen pleasures abound
Sunshine, warmth, accomplishment melding
Nature and man — one at last
Peace found

Ignorance

Never held in love's embrace
Never coddled, never cuddled
No secrets confessed
No tears of understanding
No hand reaching out

Deprived of Life's treasures
That must be unearthed
Savored, honored, felt
Or buried in the unknown
Ignorance is NOT bliss!

Birthright

Peaches and cream wrapped in soft white
Asleep in a navy blue convertible pram
While an English nanny proudly displays
This little soul, pretending to be its mother

The baby whimpers and is soothed by a pacifier
Loving arms and a bottle whose heat is tested
By a few drops spilled on the caregiver's wrist.
Gurgling sounds and loud burps soon follow

But on the other side, a tiny frail newborn
With ashen cheeks, sunken eyes, hungrily wails
As his weak mother tucks him inside her shawl
They lie on the dirt floor, cold air surrounding them

The camp reverberates with cries of hunger
While pain and sadness stalk the starry night
In desperation the nursemaid works overtime
To perform her duties as only she can

Missing Childhood

Where did my childhood go?

Is it hidden inside the blue-eyed bride doll
Sitting on the oversize maple dresser?

Is it asleep on the mahogany sleigh bed
In my enormous noisy bedroom?

Is it hiding inside one of my coloring books
Brought home as a special treat for being good?

Is it only a ghost in my colorless memory
Enigmatic, haunting my present with unreality?

Or is a rainbow peeking through the daily gray
Infusing NOW with the beauty of its interpretation?

Silence

Silence tiptoes on feathery feet
Gentle, quiet, inducing deep sleep
Standing nearby with night's protection
Then departing from Dawn's rejection

To meadows, lakes, snow-capped peaks it flies
Embraced by ever-tranquil white skies
Weightless infusion in deepest disguise
Silence pirouettes before blind eyes

Silence tiptoes on feathery feet
No one knows its arrival or retreat
All around it waits to be heard
In tones resembling emptiness, slurred

When we accept its entrance
Relax, retreat, sink into ourselves consciously
Accept with loving arms what it truly means
Then Silence co-exists with its screams

Silence tiptoes on feathery feet
Throughout the cottage and doesn't retreat
Often present day and night
No need is there to nourish or delight

Simply being there
Existing away from touch
Understanding, comforting many overwrought souls
Welcoming them with quiet sleep

Keeping their nightly world
Calm with silent relief
Returning troubled souls to sanity
May the powers of Silence always be!

REFLECTIONS
ON
REVELATIONS

Revelations

Color, texture, form, style
A flick of the wrist
A turn of oil pastel

Revelations of inner hell

Instructive choices of complementary shades
Lines straight, slanted, or figure eights
All hold meaning
Discovery the key

Revelations of inner hell

The heart has spoken
Through artistic elements
Passion existing fiercely
The spirit unbroken

Revelations of inner hell

Wheel of Life

The wheel of Life spins around
The world of feelings
Love, peace, empathy, grace
Where devotion lives in perfect space

The wheel of Life spins around
Human frailty
Hate, greed, jealousy, scorn
From which destruction will be born

The wheel spins round and round
A random landing on black or white
Ignoring those shades of gray
Which rarely come into play

The wheel spins on and on
Controlling every man's fate
Casually dropping its blurry ball
On challenges that are faced by all

Justification

The Tribunal of "Successful People"
Wishes you to justify your failures
To this point in your life

You were a teacher —
Why were you not a principal?

You went to university —
Why did you not get a Masters degree?

You took summer courses —
Why didn't you change your subject?

You taught English —
Why did you stop teaching?

You wrote poetry —
Why did you not publish a book?

You like money —
Why didn't you work more?

We, the success stories of our era
Will never understand why
Will you?

I am an Island unto Myself

I am an island unto myself
This world has nothing I can't provide
Good food, fine clothes, sports car, career
I have it all; I am rich inside

Yes, I can see that you own your own home
And you dine at the best bistros each night
Your wardrobe is chic, your car much admired
Your career's a success, but you lack insight

Who wants a wife, children, added stress?
My perfect life would become a mess!
I have it all, I am truly content
I don't want to share my life's events

What about caring and loving a mate?
Is it too hard to leave your single state?
Living on Life's surface, not inside
Is exactly what you have described

I don't need problems or disappointments
When I delight in my own enjoyment
I'm at ease in my world, happy as can be
My life is complete, can't you see?

But how can you say you've really lived
Unless you've cared, laughed, and cried?
How can you know how it truly feels
To love another from deep inside?

You haven't convinced me yet, but I'll think
And now it's time to go out for a drink
My date is waiting; she is one of a kind
I'll mull this over and then make up my mind

Yoga-1

Energy flows, angel wings relax
As Breath silently takes control
Inhale, exhale
Waves of innate circadian rhythm
Eyes close, nothing is
But All is One

Yoga-2

Surrender thoughts, motion
To undiscovered spheres
To crimson wounds
To black self doubt
To gray apathy

On hands and knees
Crawl through
The sea of thorns
The flood of tears
Clarity awaits

Full Circle

I've come full circle; now I can see
The truth of my life is what's happened to me
I've many regrets but what can I say
To change what's past and swept away?

Like clouds floating by on a windy morn
I've seen light and dark; each looked with scorn
Upon a soul that had so much to learn
But could only one lifetime allow me to discern

What was eternally good, pure, true, right?
What made me sleep or toss in the night?
What allowed me to inhale joy or grief?
I know one lifetime was all too brief

Exit

Enter right
Exit left
Exit by aisle twelve
The exits are well-marked
Know your nearest exit
Follow the arrows to exit

Only *that* exit is final

Soup Philosophy

Too much salt and in the garbage I'll be found
Too much pepper and sneezes abound
Too much water and I'm tastelessly thin
Too much flour, just imagine the shape I'll be in

Too much garlic brings social isolation
Too many onions bear the same relation
Too many tasters each with an opinion
Too much of anything and I lose my dominion

Greatness

Clasping a fragile, dying hand
Speaking to all with love and respect
Writing for those who are unable
Reading a novel to one who is blind
Praising the accomplishments of another
Singing a ditty to a restless child
Helping another, the most noble intent
Greatness lies within you

Elephantine Progress

The dreary mud-encrusted skin
Wrinkled by virtue of birth
Possesses its own army of insistent flies
Who refuse to abandon their noisy task

The massive trunk, absorbed by visitors
Who have stayed far too long
Still sweeps to and fro
Stirring the steam of a sub-tropical noon

But in spite of flies and heat
The creature lumbers forward
Deliberately, gracefully
One huge imprint at a time

No one comprehends the enormity
The elephantine grace needed
To co-ordinate all elements
But worse, no one cares

I

I breathe
I talk
I eat
I feel

I dance
I creep
I flee
I steal

I try
I struggle
I succeed
I lie

I live
I love
I write
I die

REFLECTIONS

ON

NATURE

Country Pace

Slow moving lanes
From the city to the country
Lead to a more tranquil place

A place where there is no time
A place where birds sing and nature reigns
A place for peaceful retreats

Starry skies dot the night
A glistening lake mesmerizes
English gardens please

Oh, country peace, change of pace
Lazy days and languishing nights

I glean from this heavenly kingdom
That the world is my oyster

Earthly Heartbeat

Earthly heartbeat
Essence of life
Pulse of ancient drums
Beating firmly
In circadian time
Beside the breath
Of the tropical sea

A Leaf is Life

Paws of the nightly prowler
Reach into all corners
Furtively searching
For the morsel that will entice him
To relish this tasty night

Alas! No such luck!
Only a bag filled with leaves
Gold, rust, green, dead, alive
The green feels soft, tastes acrid
But its life force satisfies the empty belly of another

Beach Rhythm

Dawn's gradual infusion
Reveals two matchstick figures
Strolling along the watery edge

As gray displaces indigo
Eager feet etch powdery sand
With their unique impressions

Some march purposefully
Others stumble
Rolling like ancient wooden wheels

Soft yellow light transforms the moment
As grains of time
Inevitably become the past

Pink, azure, sunset
The artistry of day's end
Its descent inevitable

Bubbles

Champagne sophistication fizzes
In a slender flute
Bubbles tickle the nose
Sip this touch of paradise

Relax, stare into a pond
Bubbles rise to the surface
Telling of hidden mysteries
Grudgingly confessed

Blow bubbles into the air
Watch them glide, lift and fly
Don't fret when they pop
As others will follow

Escape into the wonder of now
Let the senses luxuriate
Candles, soft music, a bubble bath
And dreams of tomorrow

Ocean

The voice of the ocean
Chants its own tune
In and out
Back and forth
Under the spell of the moon

Waves a heartbeat, white caps a result
Crusty sand, broken shells
Grainy prints along the edge
Sunshine beams over the scene
The voice breaks, its breath expires

Beams

Sunbeams through trees in early morning
Shine down on God's earthly treasures
Silent beauty of the moment

Light filtering through branches
Awes and astonishes
With miraculous fragile weightlessness

Moonbeams more delicate
Equally wondrous
The night's display of ethereal pleasure

Rainbows, prisms of color
Brief opalescence
A fleeting instant etched in heart and mind.

Crystal

Crystal suspended in the afternoon sun
Hues of raw color
Reflecting on gray walls and stucco ceiling

Crystal perfection, beauty ravishing
Shape eternal
Its origin sand

From Nature's simplicity
Universal beauty exists
Within the core of Mother Earth

Colour Power

Hot pink, lime green
Orange, cherry red
Intense hues impact eyes and head
Some love bright
Yet in evening wear
Most prefer shades of night

Should a scarlet gown appear
Drama at the ball arrives
Many an admiring comment
To it relates; the blacks
Seem washed out or without flair

If a senorita prefers hot pink
Heads turn to admire her exuberance
And unusual color sense
Alas! There's nothing on the rack
Like an orange spring suit
To give boring winter grays a boot

In summer wardrobes lime green Is a must
For swimsuits or casual wear
This shade will attract summer stares
To enjoy these tones think of fruit
Wear them proudly and bask in the envy
Of others dressed in navy suits

Autumn favors earthy tones and styles
Of gold, taupe, chocolate, beige, rust
In casual wear they are a must
Soft wool sweaters, corduroy jeans in front of the fire
What could be better?

Icicle

I can by droplets grow
Until I stretch my torso so low
That danger lurks below

I create a glossy winter scene
And with my rigid frigid form
I only crack; my life is torn

Rain

A quiet repose
A time to reflect
A cleansing moment
A refreshing refrain

Droplets on the roof
A reassuring voice
Is this man's wish
Or simply God's choice?

The greens become alive
The earth has a glow
Their gifts upon us
They surely bestow

Metamorphosis

The sands of time
Expose its passage
Along with it
Change for all species

Embryo to human
Caterpillar to butterfly
Duckling to swan
Infant to elder

Metamorphosis
Essence of life
Internal force
Unbridled energy

Cosmic miracle
To all who comprehend
Enigma
To the unenlightened

Squirrels in Spring

One April day the earth was still winter hard
When a skinny squirrel stalked the neighbor's yard
Searching for any scrap, any morsel, any taste
Of festive delights, so they'd not go to waste

This little creature wore no rodent's disguise
She saw the sad truth in his desperate eyes
Quickly the solution came into her heart and head
She could only leave him crackers, not any bread!

When she placed the salty treats on the ground
The squirrel attacked them like a bloodhound
Others waited patiently in the leafless trees
For their turn to enjoy tasty morsels like these

Soon it was easy for her to understand
That there was a famine in her own land
The furry black squirrel always arrived first
Then his underlings came and ate till they burst.

The saga of the crackers spread far and wide
Other neighbors followed suit; the squirrels had no pride
That year they knew those snacks went to a good cause
For the squirrels sat up and gave a round of applause

Time

Time to lie down
Time to disconnect
From the outside world

Time to ponder
Time to write
A poem or journal

Time to breathe
Time to inhale
The magnificence of Nature

Time to relax
Time to work
Time to contemplate
TIME

REFLECTIONS

ON

RELATIONSHIPS

Change of Heart

I welcome you with open arms
Into my home, my warm hearth
A sweet and tea, an ear to listen
Kindness, friendship, acceptance

But now I've changed

I ignore you, lock my doors
Cross my arms in frigid disgust
Save my cake for another
Whose ear and mine are symbiotic

Loveshare

Before the tempest of trouble
Enters your happy home
Before life changes
In an instant of blackness
Before the words
Can no longer be uttered
Confess your love

Mother and Child

I watch my child
Agony in my heart
With a smile plastered on my aging face

I watch my child
In his relentless battle against suffering
His fragility endures

I watch my child
His pale cheeks hollow
As he tries to hide his pain from me

I watch my child
In the arms of sleep
Hope and fear continue their battle inside

Storms and People

As menacing clouds gathered overhead
The couple exchanged angry glances
The sky began to darken
The husband refused to compromise
The rain began to fall
Tears began to flow
The downpour intensified
She shook with sobs
Thunder detonated in the sky
The words were degrading
As lightening blindly flashed

The shock of Truth was clear
The storm began to subside
Her tears shook her body
The rain became a drizzle
She slowly became silent
The sun began to appear
A silence crept into the room
The rainbow quickly formed
They asked forgiveness of each other
The storm passed

Between Love and Hate

In two different zones
Of the same realm
Lie conflicting fates --
Blessings and curses

In two different hearts
Of the opposite gender
Lie warring emotions --
Love and hate

In two different souls
Of one family
Lie opposing reactions --
Acceptance and rejection

Between two zones
Between two hearts
Between two souls
Lies the bridge of understanding

Girlfriends

Sorrows shared, frustrations aired
Laughter, tears, passage of years
Pajama parties, popcorn, Smarties
Tiffs, hugs, cottages, bugs!
Photo albums, chewing gum
First dates, zits, fancy hair clips
Graduation, celebration, infatuation
All this awaits as girlfriends relate
Lifelong friends, precious gems

Girlfriends forever

Human Interaction

A smile, a hello
A proffered hand
Eye contact
Activation of thoughts
Flow of words
Meeting of minds
Sharing of hearts
Warmth and trust

The perfect package of prerequisites
For human interaction
Nothing else required

Blind

I rejoice in the heat of your being
Your essence resonates inside my soul
My lashes thick with warm tears

No longer am I chained by the image
I confront Truth with new vision
Drastically altered by the hand of Fate

I rely on the freedom of darkness
To redesign my senses
I rejoice, shivering in your touch

As I inhale your scent
As I taste your kisses
As I listen to your words
I am overflowing with sightless ecstasy

Sexercise or Exercise?

What will it be tonight, my love, my dear?
A run in the park, a bike ride ensemble?
Or hugs and kisses to welcome the New Year?

What will it be tonight, my sweet?
A steak or oysters for your treat?
After the feast, let's bask in the heat

What will it be tonight, chérie?
Togetherness of our flesh
Or simply "We'll see?"

Yes, my love, my dear, ma chérie
We'll have it all, but you must be free!
First a run, then a bike ride, you and me
Then steak and oysters, as many as can be
I will kneel beside you on bended knee
Gorge on chocolate truffles, if you agree
At last we'll rediscover who we used to be
If you dare, then leave the rest to me!

Communication

I speak from the womb
I hear as your soft voice caresses my soul
Intoning, knowing who, what, where we are
And why we are here or there
Depending on our view, our smell, our taste of each other
As far back as when the first soul took root
And sang with its own voice to all
Who will follow in the womb of the mothers of the planet?
I speak softly so all can understand

Frustration

You said, I didn't
You denied, I affirmed
You manipulated, I complied
You refused, I accepted

You negated, I hoped
You belittled, I ignored
You destroyed, I restored
You are indifferent; I am humiliated

I am enlightened, you are unchanged
I am the student, you are the teacher
I am decisive, you are unmoved
I remember, you forget

The Touch

Gentle hands brush soft cheeks
Warmth of another's energy
Is transmitted in a white flash

Received like an electric shock
It becomes a smoldering ember
Inside red hot; outside steaming

The touch lingers beneath
Then suddenly it vanishes
Leaving only mystery in its wake

Harmony

Is it possible to live in harmony
And sing life's parts joyfully?
Can each of us ebb and flow
As we need to come and go?
Detached or together
Can harmonious moments
A blissful existence engender?

Are we two halves of a whole?
Or two melodic combinations
Spinning out of control?

Are we alive on a rewarding path?
Or is there inside an irreparable wrath?

But Who Is She?
A Tribute to a Special Lady

Who is this lady who always says "Hi"
While on the Stairmaster at the Y?
Who is this female who lifts weights
 And is admired by all in good or bad shape?

Who is this lady who circles the track
While talking to others – Yackety-yack?
Her warm heart and welcoming smile
Endear her to all through many a mile

But WHO IS this paragon of wit and grace?
Is she a shadow in time and in space?
Does she really exist in our group of friends?
Or is she a filament of dreams without end?

I think I have discovered the absolute truth
Her existence IS mortal, for I am her sleuth
Her name is Gal Pal and she is my confidante
I honor our friendship; she, my needs and wants

Now all is known about the sum of her parts
It's time to wish from the bottom of my heart
The most wonderful of days, a year of treasures
To a gal whose friendship is dear beyond measure

I Ignore

Misfortunes, negativity
Fires, tornados, disputes
Indecision, stupidity, arrogance
All in the world of a day

I Remember

I remember being hugged by my father
Holding two different hands at the same time
Eating nutritious meals I didn't like
Noises awakening me in the early morning
Being led back to my bed by a strange hand
Waking up to only half my former world

I Embrace

I embrace my dear ones when we meet
I embrace a long lost relationship
I embrace all members of my family
I embrace the triumph of creativity
I embrace a soft white teddy bear
I embrace my world and its imperfections

Kisses

With a feather dusting of kisses
Resentment abates
Anger disappears
Jealousy is overcome
Hatred is vanquished
Indifference is denied
Fear is overwhelmed
Guilt is forgotten

With a feather dusting of kisses
Trust is restored
Faith is renewed
Vigor is rejuvenated
Apathy is negated
Interest is rediscovered
Silence is broken
Love is reborn

My Chosen One

Under the stars that dot the night sky
Into a world so very different from mine
You arrived and I was soon to know
That we would see those same stars glow

You touched my heart and I believed
That you were chosen just for me
And I for you; such is our destiny
No other path need be conceived

I look at you; you look at me
I hold you in my arms
We create our own unique sphere
Mother, child, our future, my dear

Our lives now intertwine
We face forward, hand in hand
Our destiny to simply be together
You are a part of me

I softly hum Brahms lullaby
As the stars twinkle in our night sky
You grasp a lock of my dark hair
Then I whisper a thank you prayer

The Path

Walking along the narrow path

Alone

Encountering

Inadequacy
Jealousy
Rage
Along its thorny way

All this at an early age

Later, learning to hide ugly feelings
Masking them with false social veneer
Giving others the impression
Of complete escape from fear

In middle age
Change occurred
As youthful vision disappeared

Self-discovery now a personal manifest
Noticing positive change
No longer existing
As a soul
Adrift

The path now fills with others
Leading to a magical forest pool

Youthful suffering
Now fully surrendered

Here
Peace
Harmony
Contentment

Await

Every Woman's Story

Inside all female hearts and minds
Quietly lay different life experiences
Some, at a young age, triumphed
Over misfortune, disaster, poverty, loneliness
Yet others, seemingly blessed
Have had only smooth sailing in calm waters
With ever present sunny skies
Those who have endured great challenges from birth
Know well the luxury of a pain-free existence
The joy of no debt
The love of simple things
The gift of friendship
The pride of self-reliance
All supported by optimistic faith in the future

Others still have much to learn about the weather

REFLECTIONS

ON

WHIMSY

An "Omic" Tale

"My dear, did you ever witness such histrionics?"
"Never, my love; could its cause be gastronomics?"

His expressions were most certainly tragicomic
But the sound of his voice was clearly monotonic

Did you think his utterances palindromic?
No, his expertise is only taxonomic

So, why all the irrational anatomics
It must be a simple matter of economics!

One-Way Conversation

She walks, she talks
She informs, she balks
She berates, she states
She worries, she hurries
She declares, she shares
She shouts, she pouts

She walks, she talks
She ignores, she bores
She isolates, she relates
Herself, the subject
Others, her listeners
Her ignorance, her bliss

Calico Elephant

I spied you twice, yet passed you by
Tiny calico elephant in the market
But your spirit called me back each time
And as iron to a magnet
My hand reached out
To your chubby china torso
To your upturned trunk
To your upright posture
To your huge pink ears
To your striking individuality

You, the unique invention
Of unknown gifted hands
Now sit where you inspire me

Watercolor Whispers

The watercolor whispered to the portrait in oil
"Poor old you, all covered in dust and soil"
The oil responded in her sticky, squeaky tone
"But I know my place; I never moan and groan"

The watercolor turned to the dainty photograph
"You're only black and white; I look at you and laugh"
"You have a point," replied the frail black and white
"But your tones are fading with time and light"

Now the watercolor screamed to the acrylic on the floor
"You deserve your place right beside the basement door"
"I'm fine," replied the acrylic. "But are you aware
That you're in the sale today, so say a little prayer!"

Amethyst Miracle

Ageless mountain rock face
Its secrets harshly revealed
By dogged picks and axes
Extracting its raw beauty

Purple treasure resists
But finally succumbs
Eons of movement create
Violet, mauve, lavender

Utah secrets painfully revealed
By probing picks, defiant detonation
Raw beauty enthusiastically extracted
From mystic mountain rock

Violet, lavender, mauve
Grudgingly appear
Their primeval origin
An eternal mystery

Colorful

Think of happiness in color
What stands out?
Hot pink, bright red, purple, lime green
Colors that shout it out!
For these are THE BRIGHTS!

Colors that an uplifting spirit ignites
Shades that appease color-starved eyes
Hues that make the world realize
The POWER of COLOR
To positively affect one's state of mind

Here's to women and THE BRIGHTS!
May we often behold your presence
For our lives are happier
When filled with colored delights

Maud

Chiseled face of the lumberjack's wife
Testimony to a harsh, outdoor life
Rough hands, expressionless face
Colorless eyes blink into space

Red-checked apron, replete with holes
Protects the chest seared by hot coals
Faded jeans hide a skeletal frame
Filthy wet boots shielding feet inflamed

A smoker's cough from tobacco addiction
Back teeth missing, life's cruel affliction
Odors of sweat, liquor in equal parts
The overall portrait wilderness art

Soap Bubbles

Transparent, weightless spheres
Waft effortlessly in the air
Until suddenly a noiseless pop –
Droplets vanish into space

Bathtub bubbles blown blissfully
Float freely, fearlessly, overhead
Their sojourn brief but fun
Above they join lost friends

Bubbles on dishes in the sink
Know the duty that must be done
Their time limited, strength intense
Until their fate is decided

Fashionistas

Black dress, white pearls
Low heeled leather pumps
Ladies' luncheons, afternoon teas
Cucumber sandwiches, petit fours
Chatter, gossip, did you know?

No, I didn't know, for in my world
Black dresses and white pearls
Spelled funerals, even iced
With freshly coiffed, sprayed hair
Tsk, tsk, you know I must be slow
To understand the nuance, the RULE

White dress, black pearls
Open-toed flat leather sandals
The tropics gently kiss my cheeks
As I twirl under Tahitian stars
Echoes of the other life
Bless my naked back and free spirit

Lost Teddy

Teddy, oh Teddy
Without your reassuring presence
Empty is my childhood heart
In vain I search for you
But you are forever lost
Alone in middle age
With my secrets
With my insecurities
With my memories
Without you

Modern Age

Instant e-mail
Instant oatmeal
Y2K bugs
Interfaith marriage
Same-sex marriage
Test tube babies
AIDS, TB, STD'S
Train wrecks, plane crashes
Car accidents, bus tragedies
Microwave dinners
Lean Cuisine
Shipoos, cockapoos, llasapoos
Angel wisdom, cherub power
Meditation, revelation
Relaxation, renovation
Spiritual renewal
Boozing, cruising, schmoozing
High decibel lives
Heart attacks, bad backs
Depression, obsession
Anorexia, bulimia, anemia
Alimony, palimony . . .

I ask myself
Who am I?
What am I doing here?

Channel Hopping

If I am in need of a Guiding Light
To lead me through my problems
With the Young and the Restless in my life
Then I must turn to All My Children
To help sort everything out
Before a visit to General Hospital is necessary
And before Oprah and Dr. Phil
Figure out the solutions to my problems
Or Larry King and CNN broadcast everything worldwide
If Money Matters and Style hear about me I'm cooked
Like one of Martha's grain fed chicks
Will I Win a Million from Regis?
Or worship The Shopping Channel?
Or simply be a penniless Survivor
Of the Australian Outback?
Or must I visit Sally Jesse or Montel
Holding no red rose but lost hope
For solving the whole damn thing?
Maybe The Price was Right after all

Be

Be brave, be yourself
Be happy, be grateful
Be a good sport
Be clean, be kind
Be helpful, be neat

Don't be a tattletale
Don't be a fool
Don't be so sure
Don't be cruel
Don't be jealous

Know when
To be or not to be

Anticipation

The mind heats up
The heart beats up
The soul looks up
The time speeds up

Wheels down
Wind down
Chow down
Sun down

Wake up
Surf's up
Eat up
Live it up!

Beauty's Breath

A baby's smile, a puppy's devotion
A child's kiss, a mind in motion
Beauty's breath wafts everywhere

A thoughtful gesture, a work of art
Fresh hot soup in a pot, a quiet heart
Beauty's breath wafts everywhere

Scent of roses in a crystal vase
A visit from a butterfly
Beauty's breath wafts everywhere

The first touch of lovers' hands
The heroic rescue of a human life
Beauty's breath wafts everywhere

The Casserole Club

When I am no longer here
You will be wined and dined, my dear
Eligible females from far and wide
Will show a sympathetic side

Up and down each side of the street
The casserole club will bring many a treat
Some will be gourmet, high end, très cher
Others will be unadorned, of simplicity rare

But, my love, be careful of the synthetic smiles
Of the members of this club who have much to disguise
At first you may be the darling, the one pursued by all
But don't get too spoiled; you'll pay dearly for their call

Thus from afar, remember your dearest spouse
Who never brought a casserole into the house
Now you understand the reason for this lack
I knew that later they'd arrive back-to-back!

Once

Once I was a little girl
Fat cheeks pinched
Hugged and kissed
By family friends
Aunts, uncles, cousins
It was easy to be noticed
Told I had grown taller
Assured that I resembled
My father or mother
Depending on whom
I was with at the time

Once I was a young wife
Slim cheeks blushed
Pecked and hugged
By elders frail with age
Told I was looking well
That my son resembled me
Parents no longer mentioned
My status ignored by all

Now I am middle-aged
Face slightly wrinkled
Am told I don't look fifty-two
By those now ancient
Those remaining few who knew me
As a chubby child with parents
Either mother or father
Whom I resembled

Aruba

Aruba, Aruba
You remain in my soul
Your ocean so gentle
Your waters so warm
Your beaches so clean
Your shells so fine
Your sunsets so magnificent
As they disappear in time
Your lifestyle so simple
Your welcome so sincere
Your breezes so pure
Caress like cashmere

I float in your oceans
I sing in your pools
I rest on your beaches
I abide by your rules
I collect endless treasures
From your friendly seas
I watch others enjoying
Your gifts with ease
I pray for the time
I can return to your shores
I hope to reopen
Your magical doors

Mischief Maker

I'm a sweet old lady with a wicked sense of humor

I prowl nightly with my vodka, at least that's the rumor

I devour ice cream and pickles, it is reported

They suspect I'm pregnant — I must appear distorted

I love to wield my broomstick at the young

Thus my reputation as a witch on every tongue

I smoke and drink, and there's many a man

Who likes to have his way with me if he can

If I'm still in my corset, there's a battle to endure

For size 20 squashed in size 12 makes him unsure

Ah, but each day new victims I torment

Even the landlord to whom I pay my monthly rent

I forgot to mention my weekly soirees

I blast rock and roll until dawn breaks Sunday

This quiet place sorely needs a dame of my stature

So that those living here may feel the same rapture

I Wear My Zits With Pride

I wear my Zits with pride
For who at the age of fifty-six
Can still sport three Zits?
I love it when they visit me
And remain three days

When someone my age says
You're too old to have Zits
I reply that I must still be
Too young for them to leave

"How unsightly," they reply
And I laugh secretly inside
For they can only see outside
My cheeks, my nose, my chin

Oh, what terrible shape I'm in
AT MY AGE, such a shame!
I think I'm doing well, thank you
I'll wear my Zits with pride!

A Rock is Just a Rock

A rock is just a rock — or is it?
Perhaps it represents the places we visit
Brown, black, pink, gray
Are the rocks I often uncover
When on a foreign beach I stray
But a green rock is unique
In my wonderful collection
Green from the rain forest
Keeps clear my recollections
Smooth, lovely, Nature's gift to man
Reminding me of that unforgettable time
In a South American forest clan
Green supplements my worldly collection
Of sand, rocks, shells
Examining my treasures
Reminds me of Mother Nature's
Magnificent sights and smells
Gathering more rocks, sand and shells
From all over is my future goal
More travel soon beckons me
Lover of discovery!

Impossible Help

Fat, eat, nibble, crunch
Obese, help, gulp, munch
Anorexia, celery, fat, scale
Bulimia, bathroom, hide, fail
Logic, sweat, thought, isolation
Irrationality, smell, abhorrence, desolation

Help, counsellor, doctor, nurse
Lifesaver, IV, dietitian, curse
Family, desperation, breakdown, finality
Friends, loyalty, adjustment, actuality

Hospital, cure, despair, tragedy

FINGERNAILS

Long, elegant, manicured in pink
Some fingernails never touch water and a sink!
Short, stubby, bitten to the quick, sore
These nails really need much more
Chipped, raw, peeling, neglected
These nails are lucky they're not infected

Clean, polished, clear, short
These nails are cared for, yet full of sport

Black, blue, yellow, green
All on 5 nails
Show that the lady's taste
Is surely derailed

Next time at lunch with your friends
Notice their nails!

REFLECTIONS

ON

LIFE

Creativity

What can I do well, I often ponder
The answer lies in my unique style
A mysterious word unmasked
A verbal challenge taken to task
A delicious rounded poetic soufflé
A soothingly sweet prose parfait

Words to savor, words to share
Words to create a unique prayer
Words to lighten a heavy heart
Words to join hearts formerly apart
Words to master, words to entwine
Words that are temporarily mine

With words, the tools of my trade
I am their surgeon, daily I operate
The power to change sadness to mirth
Lies in my pen and proves my worth
Thus I evolve through my words
My doubts, fears no longer heard

Free Form Ballet

Point the toe, flex the foot
Circle left, circle right
Repeat other leg

The barre is unforgiving
Lift the right leg, stomach in
Bend from the hip, exhale
Repeat other side

Now you've earned the right
To move as you wish, within reason

Mental Laundry Day

Sort your troubles into lights, darks,
    And delicates
Make certain each is kept
    With its own kind
Use the appropriate detergent and water temperature
    For each pile
Rinse thoroughly and either hang in the sun to dry
    Or use the dryer
Don't over dry; don't stretch out delicate fabrics
    By hanging too long
Fold or hang on suitable hangars so that
    The items lay correctly
Sort your troubles into piles -- minor, major
    And life threatening
Make certain to keep them
    In proper perspective
Use the appropriate method to deal with each type
    Depending upon its severity
Understand that it takes time
    To resolve an issue
Surrender the problem to God; discuss with a friend
    Or meditate until the answer reveals itself
Don't obsess; relax and let time gently lead you
    To the resolution
When the issue is resolved, mentally fold it up
    And put it away in your drawer of experience
Move forward with new awareness
    This laundry is done!

The Poet and the Painter

I, the poet; she, the painter
Give birth to reflective realms
Artistry of thought and brush
Shape rare complementary images
Our paths cross, merge, unite
To create Beauty, that magical force
Pushing and pulling words and colors
In different but fulfilling directions
Each passion echoing the other
Accompanied by success, failure, frustration
I persevere into awe-inspiring magic
Exploring uncharted regions of my secret world

The Power of the Pen

I can create world peace
Or end a sacred human relationship
I can sign on the dotted line
For a car, home or cottage
I can seal one's fate in education
Marriage or career
I keep in touch with others from far and near
I cost only 50 cents
But can change the world in many ways
Never before anticipated or surmised
Did anyone ever realize
My slender power in their lives?

Life's Delights

Watercolors inspire
Oils endure
Mirrors reveal
Snow sparkles
Fingers touch
Notes resonate
Hearts discover
Love unites

The Mannequin

No aches or pains make me motionless
No wrinkles or spots cause me distress
No weight fluctuations disrupt my brain
No hormonal problems give me pain

No friends or family do I adore
No money problems shake my core
No bills, no taxes, no housework to do
No pets, no shopping, the demands are few

One day I know I'll be yellowed with age
They'll take me away, I hope to the stage
I'll become a prop and under soft lights
My youth may return to those with poor sight

Many must imagine how thrilled I am
But they don't see my life is a sham

Daily Dance

The delicate twinkle
Of guitar and harp
Infuse my early morning ears
With inspiration
As my lethargic form
Begins to conceive of and perform
Its daily dance

Body and soul connect
As the fragile Celtic melody
With its haunting spell
Works its magic
Swing of arms
Sway of hips
Tilt of head
Unfold gracefully
Until notes
Are heard no more

Eyes now sparkling
Heart quickly beating
Mind clearer
The dance evaporates

Nobody Home

I searched my cerebellum
But no tenants were at home
I hunted for my common nouns
But they chose to leave me alone

They went out with the active verbs
To find the direct objects of thought
Then the adjectives decided to dress
And join the negations nor and not

The articles moved from 'a' to 'the'
As the adverbs found their lost 'ly'
In silence all parts could now hear
The plea that had become a cry

Gerunds and participles led the parade
Returning home after their winged flight
Nouns and verbs made uncommon haste
Knowing my dilemma that helpless night

All literary legions returned by rank
The Actives led the Passive pack
As light blazed over all the parts
My arid brain found its own way back

Faceless

I am my designer's faceless face
I am of the world, of any race
I observe those who stop to see
My couturier clothes, but never me

Shielded from words I cannot hear
I stand tall and proud year after year
Observing those who glance at me
Telling friends if they like what they see

I'm the source of attention from one and all
As my clothes change weekly from Spring to Fall
From my windowed world eyes are staring
At the newest ensemble I am wearing

Suddenly the crowd resumes their pace
Determination set in many a face
Those who stop never clearly see
Who I am, what I know, the real me

The Bitter Bride

Dickens' Miss Havisham

In bridal white I waited on my wedding day
My home resplendent with nuptial display
Leaving me in humiliation and disgrace
My groom disappeared without a trace

For three painful days I awaited news
That never came to explain his views
In all eyes abandoned at the altar
My youthful confidence now began to falter

Bitterness overtook my heart and soul
To gain revenge became my exclusive goal
Magnificent draperies forever shut out
The cruelty outside, I became a recluse

As I sat at the crumbling remains
Of my now ghostly repast
In darkness and misery I devised a plan
To torture in love a young innocent man

Years flew by, my bridal dress decayed
As my clothing turned a ghostly gray
I remained in my chair, never going out
I became old, cruel, ugly, only gossiped about
Causing others to suffer as I had so long ago
In my veins only revenge would flow

Spiders, rot, mould, dust my friend
Until one day I was forced to face my end
As a nasty old woman, evil and mean
Whose life had stopped at three fifteen

The truth too much for me to bear
I trusted myself into God's loving care
But before my final sad goodbyes
I had to ask forgiveness and apologize

Soon my sadness would come to an end
Light burned my eyes, fire became my friend

Father

With simplicity as his philosophy
My silken father was MY adult king
Holding his large warm hand
Made me feel safe, important

Shades of the past
Memories now engulf me
As I find them inside

Humble, yet well-educated
In school and in Life
He was respected by all
He lived to help others

Shades of the past
Sparks of adult understanding
Intensify my thoughts

Checker games I always won
Sunday visits to my cousins
Special outings with my friends
Always there, my Father

Shades of the past

A dozen red roses at my graduation
Proudly marching me down the aisle
Loving my husband as his own son

Shades of the past

A distraught phone call in the night
Arriving too late to say good-bye
Anger enveloping my heart and soul

Shades of the past

The shock and disbelief of tragedy
The absence of someone important
In the life of my young family

Shades of the past grow longer
With each passing year

A Mother's Prayer

As I watch from the shadows
My elusive bride
Her crystal bouquet
Reflecting the summer rays
I am overwhelmed
My spirit in awe
Transfixed by the magnetic pull
Of her ethereal presence
Unique in her individuality
Yet she is Every Woman
Past and present
Stepping over the threshold
Silk slipper forward
Outwardly confident
Within lies a fragile heart
Pulsing with love
I murmur a silent prayer
For her eternal joy
While the silver circle
Sits proudly on her head

May she be eternally enveloped by loving arms
May she possess the strength to weather Life's storms
And may she always love and be loved

Mother
June 10, 2000

123

Bequest

I have decided to write for all eternity
My last will and testament
For all to enjoy after my demise

I bequeath to my middle-aged image
the following:
1) the gift of seeing herself as she is
2) the treasure of loving herself in old age
3) the charity to bestow her greatest assets
   upon the world
4) the generosity of spirit to examine her life,
   knowing that her mistakes made her human
5) the legacy of a family to carry her in their hearts
6) the wisdom to understand all of the above

Signed,

Your Mirror

About the Poet

Ellen Alban has been interested in poetry writing for the last six years. A former teacher, she now devotes her time to writing, volunteer work, yoga, dance, and friends and family. Most of her poetry is based on her personal view of the world, its people and the little things in life that, when given notice, become memorable and important.

ISBN 1-41204375-1